Down From Heaven

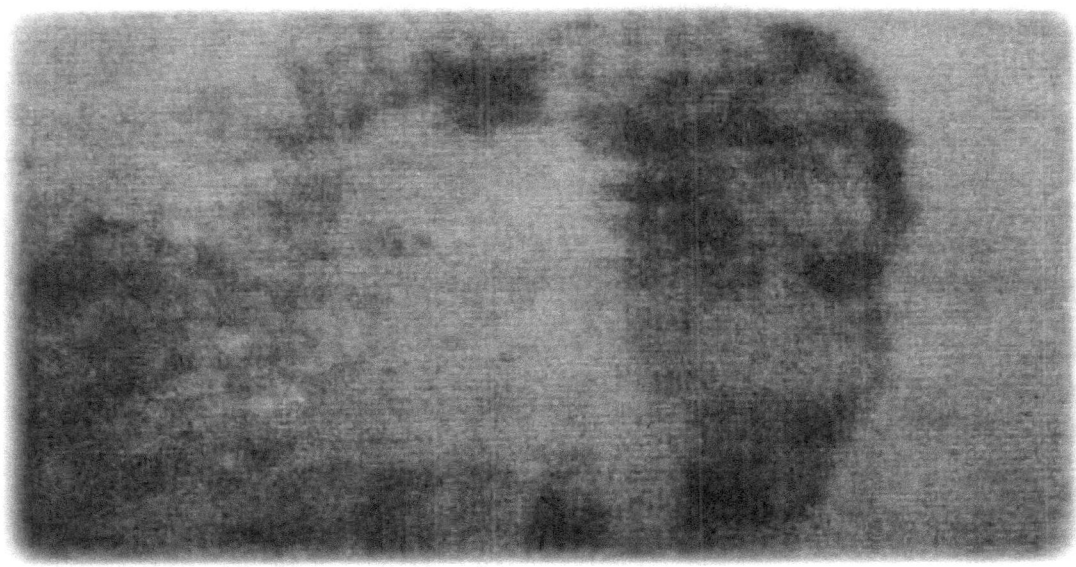

"The Kingdom"
of Heaven is at hand

Pastor Maverick Vera

Copyright © 2016 Maverick Vera

Cover Design © 2016 Matthew Hoflund

Cover Photo © Maverick Vera. All rights reserved.

All rights reserved. No part of this book may be reproduced in any form or by any means — graphic, electronic, or mechanical, including photocopying, recording, taping, or information storage and retrieval systems — without written permission of the publisher.

Copyright © 2016 Maverick Vera

All rights reserved.

ISBN-10: 0997577908

ISBN-13: 978-0997577907

Printed in the United States of America

Contents

Introduction

1. The River
2. The Ring
3. Construction
4. Big Rock
5. Plastic Flower
6. Box From Mom
7. The Cup
8. Watering The Seeds
9. The Tree That Fell
10. War
11. The Beauty of Things
12. Repentance
13. The Door
14. The Fire
15. The Bread
16. The Power of the Word
17. Minister
18. Our Neighbor
19. Obedience
20. The Town
21. The Lost Boy
22. Faith
23. The Face of Jesus

Acknowledgements

Introduction

Spiritual Guidance from our Christian Church

A letter From Maverick

This is based on a true story. If you believe, GOD bless you, and if you do not, GOD forgive you. Because that's the truth and there's nothing I can do about that. Maverick Vera was born, and grew up in Honolulu, Hawaii in the year 1959, and resides there currently. Back in the late 1980's on one stormy morning, I was in a room facing the mountain. I heard a voice talking to me, telling me to do some things. I questioned who was talking to me, I said out loud, "If you are the GOD of Abraham, Isaac and Jacob, I will do whatever you want me to do. But I will ask you GOD, one thing in return. I would like a picture of your son Jesus that I can hold in my hands. From that time on I was told many things.

When friends were making repairs on my roof, sometimes it would rain very hard. The rain would come into the house in through the ceiling. The water had made a stain on the ceiling leaving a water mark. One morning when I woke up I looked at the stain. I saw the face of Jesus, He had a crown of thorns and blood on his head. There were three different faces on the other side. I then remembered about five years ago what I asked for. (This is the photograph I used on the front cover; this photograph, "The Face of Jesus" is also available as a high quality print at: www.MaverickVera.com)

Miracles still happen.

    Since I was a little boy, I knew, like many others, that there was something watching over us. The things around us were made to be so perfect; the air, the water, the trees. All things were full of enjoyment in life.   There was also another side where I was lost, or had lost a friend, family, or someone I loved.

Questions needed to be answered, and there was a voice in my heart. Why did some things happen this way, and who was in control? The only thing I was looking for was the truth. These things can't be found in many people, but is the real reason to what life is all about. I found myself looking in the Bible sometimes, maybe trying to find something for the pain in my heart. And there I found hope and comfort in the word of God. Most of all I found the truth.

Now, for all the things that was given to me, I will give in return my time helping, teaching, and praying, and to also build a church. This is all for the kingdom of GOD.

There comes a time in everyone's life when there is doubt. Feelings of inadequacy can taint all that is touched. Unfortunately it is at these times when we tend to question our faith and demand proof from God that he is still with us. It is funny, it is in times of emotional turmoil when we question God's plan. For in times of joy, it is seldom doubted.

Though who are we, any one of us, to question the Lord? We accept whatever comes our way until we think that we will crumble under the strain. It is at that point where we fail to see how we are being guided. Yet it is He who made us, and it is He who helps us grow stronger in body, mind, and spirit. Our trials are His trials.

Yet, it is human nature to search for something tangible to hold onto in times of great need. No matter how strong our faith is, sometimes our own imperfection is daunting. It may be that self-doubt can loosen ones faith. However, feelings of unworthiness don't make us unworthy of His Love. It just makes us human and fallible just as he made us.

It is during one of the darkest hours I had ever faced that God chose to give me one of those signs we so often search for in life. By His face, on these pages, I will show you what He has shown me.

   Though my story may not seem extraordinary in many ways, it is the event that can be found on these pages that have significantly changed my life and increased my faith forever. If, in my story, you can find some peace, hope, or inspiration in some small way, then I am happy to share it.

   Thank You for allowing Me the opportunity to share this experience with You. May God Be With You,

   - *Maverick*

Down From Heaven

"The Kingdom" of Heaven is at hand

Now, in John 3:27, it is written that John the Baptist said, **"A man can receive nothing except it be given him from the kingdom."** And when Jesus was demanded of the Pharisees, when the kingdom of God should come, He answered, **"...the Kingdom of God is within you." (Lk. 17:21)** That's also where your treasure shall be, for that is the Kingdom of God.

Parable 1
The River

Let's talk about the effects of complaining and murmuring. There was a teenager whose parents taught him about the Bible all of his life. And he was so happy. One day he was walking in the mountains, praising and singing to God.

When he came to a river, he wanted to cross it. And he saw a path of rocks that he could cross over in the river without getting his feet wet, so he started to cross. But when he had gone halfway across, he slipped and fell in the water. So he climbed out and sat on the rock on the other side. He was not pleased. He grumbled and said, "God, I know that you're always with me and you always protect me, and I always trust you; but why" he said, "why did you let me fall in the water?"

God opened the skies and said, "Why do you look down and complain of what happened to you? For at the moment you fell in the water, I had baptized you." Again, I tell you, what was thought was a curse was actually a blessing.

Phil. 2:14 - "Do all things without murmurings and disputings..."

Parable 2
The Ring

There was once a poor man who walked into a store. He saw that the owner of the store was a lady, and she was talking to her friend. And she was saying to the friend, "Look at my diamond ring. My husband bought it for me. It's so big and shiny." And her friend was saying the same words, "Look at my diamond ring that my husband bought for me. It is so big and shiny."

The poor man said, "I have a diamond ring bigger and shinier than all of you guys put together." And they asked him, "Where is it?" Then he said,

"It is the glory of God that is in my heart." The man lifted up his hands and said, "For you can see what I do not have." And he took his finger and put it to his heart and said, "But what I have you cannot see." For it is written, "The Kingdom of God is hidden from the wise and the prudent." (Lk. 10:21)

            Amen

 Mt. 6:20-21 - "...but lay up for yourselves treasures in heaven, where neither moth nor rust doth corrupt, and where thieves do not break through nor steal: For where your treasure is, there will your heart be also."

Parable 3
Construction

There was a man who worked in construction, and he was a big man like a friend of mine named Duke. People used to speak well about him. They would say, "This man is a man of God, and God lives in this man." But one day, far away, another man was watching him. And the big man lifted up his hand and struck another man.

Later on that day, the man walked up to him and said, "They said you're a man of God, and God lives in you, but I saw you strike another man." The good man held his peace. He did not say one word and walked away.

Now days after, the man went up to him again and said, "They said you're a man of God, and God lives in you but I saw you strike another man." Then he said, "Why don't you answer me?" The good man said, "Even that man at that moment couldn't answer me for he had something stuck in his throat, and he could not breathe. I lifted up my hand, struck him on his back and I said, God, give this man the breath of life again."

For what people thought was a curse, was a blessing from God; It wasn't what they saw. And the man said, "Forgive me." And the good man said, "I am also forgiven."

Mt. 7:1 - "Judge not, that ye be not judged."

Parable 4
Big Rock

There was a man who owned a house and in the front of his house there was a big rock. Every day he and his family had to go around the rock to get into his house. So one day he looked in the phone book and hired five contractors to come and destroy the rock so his family could walk into the house. So the contractors came the next day and talked about how they were going to destroy this big rock.

   And one man said, "Let's burn the rock." They replied, "It's going to take too long." He then said, "Let's put chemicals on the rock to dissolve it." Again they said, "It also would take too long." So he said, "Let's blow up the rock." And they said, "That would damage the house."

   About the same time there was a young boy walking down the street, who looked at the five wise men and said, "What is the problem you guys have? And they laughed at him and said, "The owner will pay us to destroy this rock and how is it that you, a boy, can give us the answer?" He looked at them and said, "Wait. I'll be back."

The boy left and returned with a machine called a back-ho. And he dug a big hole in the front of the rock and reached over, and pushed the rock into hole. And the men looked at him as he was going to reverse, and stopped him. They said, "Come off of the machine. We want to talk to you." They asked him, "Where did you learn to do this?" The boy said, "Have you not read the Scriptures? For the Son of God said, "I have not come to destroy the laws and the prophets, but I came to clear the way into the Kingdom of God." (Mt. 10:21) The boy said, "I have done the same."

I'll ask you one question, "What is the rock?" For the rock is like Satan. Satan is always in your way and you always have to go around him. Not one time did Jesus destroy Satan, but always told him to leave, and always put him in his place. So likewise the boy put the rock underneath the ground. And he said it's like Satan. How you can put Satan underneath your feet. And you walk over him for you have the power to do that.

Jn. 14:6 - "Jesus saith unto him, I am the way, the truth, and the life: no man cometh unto the Father, but by me."

Parable 5
Plastic Flower

I'll tell you what the love of God is. There was a man that loved his wife very much and the date was February 14th. It was Valentine's Day. This man came home from work and his wife was in the kitchen cooking. He gave her some flowers and kissed her. But when she looked at the flowers, they were made of plastic and she was wondering why her husband gave her plastic flowers and not real flowers. It was very troubling to her. At that time, he went outside and began to feed his animals and water the plants.

When evening came while they were watching TV, she turned to him and said, "I have a problem." And he said, "What is it?" She replied, "Why did you give me plastic flowers and not real flowers? Is your love for me not real? The man answered and said, "My love for you is like the Love of God." She said, "What do you mean, like the Love of God?" He said, "If I had bought you real flowers it would have lasted for two or three days, and then they would die. For the flowers I bought for you are like the Love of God—it will never die."

Then she knew the meaning of the flowers, and went up to the flowers, and brought them close to her. For now they meant a lot.

Jn. 3:16 - "For God so loved the world, that he gave his only begotten Son, that whosoever believeth in him should not perish, but have everlasting life."

Parable 6
Box From Mom

For it is written, "Thou shall love thy God with all your heart, with all your soul, with all your mind, and with all your strength." How does it feel in that way?

There was once an old lady who lived two or three houses away from her son. One day she realized it was his birthday. So when evening came, she walked to her son's house, knocked on the door, and she told him, "Happy Birthday." She gave her son a beautiful box, and when the son opened the box it was empty. So the son said, "What is this? It is empty." She said, "You could fill it up with sand, you could fill it up with water, you could fill it up with anything, but this box will always have room for my love for you.

   Now with all her strength she had, she had gone over to her son's house. With all her mind she remembered her son's birthday. With all her heart she had given her son a gift. And with her soul she gave him the only thing she had.

Now, the box is like God. No matter what you do wrong, he always has room for his love for you.

Amen.

Lk. 10:27 - "And he answering said, Thou shalt love the Lord thy God with all thy heart, and with all thy soul, and with all thy strength, and with all thy mind."

Parable 7
The Cup

For it is written, **"Offenses must come."** Now I will reveal more in this parable than I did in the others.

There was a man who had a cup and God came unto him and put things into this cup. He put love, understanding, and patience, and the gifts from God. Then God told him, "Go and share the things that I have given you." And the man went out to share his love. He also gave his understanding, but people took advantage of him. They despitefully used him and took everything he had.

When offenses came, his cup broke. And all that God had given to him fell out of the cup, and the man became a worldly man. He lost his patience. He had no love. He no longer had anything from God. So he came back to God and he asked, "God, can you please mend this cup and give me what you gave me before?" And God said, "No." Again he went to God and asked, "God, can you mend this cup and fix it to give me what you gave me before? And God said, "No." Then he said to God, "Then what shall I do?" God said, "Go build another cup, bigger and stronger than the first by the foundation of the Word."

So the man went and studied again

the foundation of the Word and afterwards built a cup which God came and filled up again with all the things that he had before, and even more because his cup was now bigger.

If you have the foundation of the Word but not the love of God inside you, it is not good. And if you have only the love of God in you without the foundation of the Word, offenses shall come and take away the love. But if you have the foundation of the Word AND the love of God in you, when offenses come, they cannot take the love of God away from you because of the foundation of the Word.

Amen.

Mt. 18:7 - "Woe unto the world because of offenses! for it must needs be that offenses come; but woe to that man by whom the offense cometh!"

Parable 8
Watering The Seeds

There once was a man who loved his wife very much and he lived with her family. And when evenings would come, he would go outside to the porch and look at the stars and the moon. And he would call his wife and say, "Please, come outside; look at the stars and the moon with me." But she would stay in the house with her mom and neglect him.

Again, the next day he would do the same and ask his wife, "Please, come outside; look at the stars and the moon with me. But she would not. She continued to neglect him.

Then one night he went outside and he said, "God, I know that if a man is married to a woman, she should be with him." So he became very hurt inside of himself. The next day he went to the store and bought a package of flower seeds. And again at night he went up to his wife and said, "Please come outside and look at the stars and the moon with me", but she wouldn't. So he went outside on the porch by himself and dug a small ditch in the ground and he put all his seeds in it and covered them up. He said, "God, if upon these seeds there is no rain, these seeds will not grow and it would be a miracle. If these seeds will grow, I'll keep my word and come back to my wife."

　　Late that night, while she was sleeping, he took all his clothes and left. In the morning when she woke up he was gone. All of his clothes were gone, and she was hurt.

　　Now when evening came again, she remembered what her husband said, "Come outside and look at the stars and the moon with me." So she went out there and thought about her husband

and her heart began to ache. She started to cry in the place where her husband used to sit. And for three or four nights she went outside and cried and cried. While she was crying, all of her tears were falling into the ground where the seeds were, and it was watering the seeds.

Now, two weeks later the man came back to the house and noticed the flowers were starting to grow. He said to God, "I shall keep my word. It's a miracle! This is great! Now I will come back to my wife."

Now why did the flowers grow? I will tell you. The woman cried, for she loved her husband. If you have love for anything, it shall grow. And without that love, things shall die.

Mt. 19:6 - "Wherefore they are no more twain, but one flesh. What therefore God hath joined together, let not man put asunder."

Parable 9
The Tree That Fell

As we all sit here, we are all Christians. Not every day will be a good day. We go through troubles sometimes. We murmur and complain sometimes.

There was a man who was cleaning his yard, and as he was kneeling down and picking up leaves, he was praying unto God. At that moment a centipede bit his hand. So he stood up and walked away, and said, "God, what have I done wrong? I've always believed that you would protect and watch over me. Why have I been punished for this?"

As soon as he said those words, a big tree fell exactly where he was standing. He turned and saw what had happened and fell down to his knees and said, "God, forgive me for I know now that you have truly loved me."

God saved his life. What he thought was a curse, was really a blessing.

Phil. 2:14 - "Do all things without murmurings and disputings."

Parable 10
War

I have told you about love, and now I shall tell you about the lack of love.

There was a man who loved this girl so much that he visited her all the time. He brought her gifts. He brought her candy. He brought her flowers. And he always told her how much he loved her.

But there was never a time that she said she loved him.

Now, the time came when there was a war in a foreign country and he enlisted into the Army. While he was far away waiting to come back, someone said, "Tomorrow we need someone to volunteer for a special assignment. Who will volunteer first?" And the man stood up and said, "I shall go first! I shall go first!" And some of those around him said, "You are a brave man." He said, "No. I have loved many women, but I have not been loved in return."

Now, at the very moment, far away, the girl that he loved was writing a letter. And for the very first time in her letter, she wrote, "I love you." But the letter didn't reach him until two or three days later. But the man lost his life by then. It wasn't by bullets or by bombs that he died. What do you suppose the man died of?

If you love somebody don't wait for tomorrow to let them know. Tomorrow may not come and, most of all, when you love somebody thank Jesus that you love Him also.

1 Cor. 13:1 - "Though I speak with the tongues of men and of angels, and have not charity, I am become as sounding brass, or a tinkling cymbal."

Parable 11
The Beauty of Things

If you don't read the Word of God, sometimes you don't recognize the things that are of God.

There was an old woman who said, "All of my life I've read the Bible and I've studied and there was not one time that I saw that there was something that happened that came into play or took place in front of me."

One day she wanted to buy a bird. So she went into a pet shop. And she saw two birds in one cage. And one bird was pretty and the other bird wasn't.

So she went up to the owner and said, "How much is this pretty bird?" He said, "It cost 30 dollars." Then she asked, "How much is the bird that's not pretty? Again, he said, "It's also 30 dollars."

But she only wanted to buy one bird, however she felt that the one bird would be lonely. So she bought both birds. When she went home and after 45 minutes to one hour, she looked at the pretty bird. She kept on staring at the pretty bird. And she thought to herself, "Was that second 30 dollars' worth my money?"

Then she went into another room, opened up the Bible, and began reading.

As she was reading, she heard a noise, it was one of the birds singing so beautifully. So she closed the Bible with one finger inside and walked up to the cage and noticed that the bird that wasn't pretty was singing so beautifully. She opened her Bible up again and read, "He that has eyes to see, let him see. And he that has ears, let him hear", for this is the beauty of God.

    When you see somebody that's not beautiful, but they might be beautiful inside; they have different talents, different things, and different gifts. Remember the poor man in the second parable? Who was the richest? For what you have on the outside, anyone can come and take it away from you. But what you have on the inside, no one can take it away from you.

Mk. 4:12 - "...that seeing they may see, and not perceive; and hearing they may hear, and not understand; lest at any time they should be converted, and their sins should be forgiven them."

Parable 12
Repentance

There was an old man who had a very large yard and some kids were cleaning the front of his yard. And he called the kids, "Come, and sit down underneath this tree." So he gave to them cookies and milk, and said to them, "I shall tell you a story." He said, "Once there was a big tree. And this tree was good in the eyes of the Lord. For this tree was so big that in all the branches, the birds would come and make their nests. And from the morning until night, the birds would sing. There was such peace and harmony. On this tree was plenty of fruit that the birds would come and eat. And the fruit that dropped underneath, the animals would eat. Now, when it rained, the animals came for shelter in and under the tree. When it was too hot, the animals had shade.

Now, in the middle of this tree was a hole. And in this hole the honeybees would put all their honey. This tree was good in the eyes of the Lord, for the fruit was sweeter than any other tree. But then one day came a person that was unjust, an evil person, who took a big bag of salt and poured it into the tree. Now slowly the tree started to die. The leaves fell and the birds flew away. When animals came for shelter, they had no shelter. When the rain came, the tree could no longer protect them from the rain.

Now as the tree was starting to die, God said, "This tree belongs to me for it is good in my eyes." So God blessed it and it rained for three days. It rained very hard and He washed all the salt away from the tree. And days afterwards, the tree came back to life."

Now there was a girl that was 13 years old that said, "I know what you're talking about, you're not talking about a tree." So the little boy who was sitting next to her pulled her back and said, "What is he talking about then?" She said, "He's talking about a person. When she was lonely, God came to her and talked peace and harmony. Just as when you are hungry, she is like the fruits of the tree, she gives you something to eat. And when it is raining, she takes you in.

And when it is too hot, she gives you shelter.

But when he talked about honey. It was like the heart of the person. If someone comes and does evil to this person, when the evil and bitterness enters the person's heart, she loses her friends, her family, her job, and everything that person has.

Now the person starts to die like that tree. But when the person repents unto God for forgiveness, like the rain that waters the tree for three days, the Holy Spirit comes into that person. He is the living water and when the living water comes into that person, all the hate goes out of that person. It was like the tree. It was good in the eyes of the Lord, for he got back with her family, her friends, and her job."

Whatever has been taken away from you by man, surely God can give it back to you.

Mk. 4:17 - "...and have no root in themselves, and so endure but for a time: afterward, when affliction or persecution ariseth for the word's sake, immediately they are offended."

Parable 13
The Door

There was a man who was looking for a woman, by the will of God. So he went and knocked on a door, and God opened the door. Then he asked, "God, is the woman I'm looking for in here?" God said, "Yes, come in and look." So he walked in and looked all over and found many women but not the one he was looking for. So he went back to God and said, "God, I have knocked and you have opened the door. I asked you and you told me "Yes." Why have you let me look and not find the woman?"

God said, "What did you find?" The man said, "I found several more doors." God said, "Then why did you knock only on the first door?" God knew that he was looking for someone special. Sometimes you've got to keep on knocking at the door. And if you knock on the door and God answers, or God gives you something, a gift from heaven, and you just have the gift, that's all you're going to have.

But if you have one gift from God, go again and ask him for another, and if he's willing, he will give you another, and another, and another gift from heaven. Keep on knocking, keep on asking and keep on seeking and you shall have the things you need. Don't give up.

Mt. 7:7-8 - "Ask, and it shall be given you; seek, and ye shall find; knock, and it shall be opened unto you: for every one that asketh receiveth; and he that seeketh findeth; and to him that knocketh it shall be opened."

Parable 14
The Fire

Judge not and you shall not be judged.

There once was a young woman she was about 30, and she had a very pretty face. She was a very simple woman. At times she didn't comb her hair, and she wore baggy clothes. In the supermarket when she used to buy things, she would pick up vegetables and fruits and would say out loud, "How can they sell these things to people, it is half spoiled!" She used to say, "How can they buy these cheap things that are so easily broken?" The people would say that something was wrong with this woman. In this small town the people used to say "Keep away from her because she is always talking to herself." Now let me tell you about this woman. One day she was in the supermarket buying groceries. Outside in the intersection there was a big accident. In the first car the people got out and they were okay, but in the other car, as soon as the people got out it burst into flames. In the backseat there were two little babies. They tried to get the babies out but the flames were too intense. The woman who was buying groceries in the store came out the front door. When she saw the car in flames, she said "Oh my God!", and she dropped her groceries. By then there was a big crowd. She ran up to the car and lifted her hands and broke the window to take the two little babies out. When she walked into the crowd, she put the two babies down, and when she walked away she looked up and said, "God, What else can I do for you?"

The peoples' hearts broke when one man said; "All the times that she was speaking she was talking to God, and we condemned her. It was us who should have been condemned." The moment this woman lifted her eyes and asked, "What else can I do for you?" she had glorified the Kingdom of God, she didn't look back to what she had done; but was again willing to work more.

Mt. 7:1 - "Judge not, that ye be not judged."

Parable 15
The Bread

To have faith, some things you cannot see.

    There once was this boy and he took three of his friends to a drive-in to get something to eat. While they were eating, the boy took some bread from his plate, and threw it on the ground. A sparrow came down and ate a lot of bread then flew away. And the boy said "It was good of me that I fed three birds. His friends looked at him and they said, "We have only seen one bird, how is it that you say that you've fed three birds?" He said, "Because you do not know the time and the seasons. For that was a mother bird, who went back and fed two other birds in the nest." Then he asked his friends, "How many birds did I feed?" They said, "It is possible that you fed three birds." Then he said, "Why then is it impossible to believe in God, who you cannot see?" They said to him, "You're always talking about your God. Teach us something about your God." He said, "God sent bread down from Heaven, called Manna. This was the bread they ate with Moses for 40 years and then they died. Now there was a different time and season that God sent bread from Heaven. This was the true bread from Heaven. The living bread. Anyone who eats of this bread, and drinks of this wine, will never die."

They said to him, "So if we just eat bread, and drink wine, we will not die?" He said, "If you just eat bread, and drink wine, you surely will die. But if you eat of **this** bread, and drink of **this** wine, which came down from Heaven, and receive it by the spirit of God, you will not die. The bread *IS* Jesus Christ.

Jn. 6:51 - "I am the living bread which came down from heaven: if any man eat of this bread, he shall live forever: and the bread that I will give is my flesh, which I will give for the life of the world."

Parable 16
The Power of the Word

For this is the power of the word, and one time there was a man; A big strong man. He went into town, and he was drinking, and he got into some trouble. He ended up fighting with 2 or 3 people in the streets, and the police officers came, and they couldn't come close to him because he was so strong, and very fast. Then they called more police officers, and now there were about 10 police officers that were there. They couldn't hold him or detain him for he was very strong. So they called the Captain. And the Captain came and said, "What is wrong here?" They said,

"This man is too strong for us, for we cannot hold him." The Captain said, "Find out who this man is, and find out who his wife is, and bring her." And they brought the man's wife, and in the crowd the man's wife spoke out. And she was a small woman, and she said, "If you Love me, then listen to me. For I Love You, and I Love You Always." The man didn't say one word. Then she told her husband, "Put your hands behind your back, and go down to your knees." And he did so. And they took him and his wife away. The officers went up to the captain and said, "How can this small woman control him? For how small she is, how can she have so much power and be so strong?" And the Captain said,

"Are you with ears, and did not hear? Or are you with eyes, and did not see? Or you are with a mind, and did not understand? For it was the power in the word." For she said, "If you Love me, then listen to me. Because I Love You, and I Love You Always." Is that not the same words that God is always telling his people? For this world came to be, even by the word.

                                                  Amen.

Mt. 8:8 - "The centurion answered and said, Lord, I am not worthy that thou shouldest come under my roof: but speak the word only, and my servant shall be healed."

Parable 17
Minister

There once was a minister who owned a construction company. As he was driving down past the store, he saw two young men standing by the store, just idling. He asked the two men if they wanted to work for a couple of hours. As they were working, he had taught them about God's things. How you are supposed to nourish your body and spirit. After two hours of working, the job was finished. He paid the young men for the time they had worked. And he dropped them back off at the store. Now one of the young men went into the store to buy milk and a sandwich, and he stood in front of the store. The other young man went to buy some beer and cigarettes. Because the beer is not legal in public, he went to the back of the store, so he could hide. Now, when the minister went home, he had another phone call for another job. So he went back down to the store to look for the two young men, and found one of the men; nourishing his body in front of the store, in the light, doing good. And the other man, he could not find, who was in the back of the store, doing wrong, in the darkness. So the minister could only pick up one of the men. When you do good, you do it in the light. And when you do wrong, you do it in the darkness.

God will reward you for the things you do in the light.

Lk. 12:2 - "For there is nothing covered, that shall not be revealed; neither hid, that shall not be known."

Parable 18
Our Neighbor

There was a young man, who always believed in God. And one day he was very, very hungry. And he only had about $3.00. Now he walked down to the store, about seven blocks, to buy something to eat. Right before he walked into the store, he saw another man sitting down by the door of the store. When he looked at this man, he felt sorrow in his heart, because he knew this man was much hungrier than he was. So he gave the man all the money that he had, and walked all the way back home.

He went into his kitchen, and grabbed some old bread. He sat down in his living room, and he started to speak. He said, "Man shall not live by bread alone, but by the things that are of God." As he started to eat the bread, tears fell from his eyes, onto the bread. Then he said, "Whatever came out of me shall go back into me." At that moment, God sent two Angels above him, and said,

"God is well pleased. Not only what you have said, but also what you have done."

Amen.

Mk. 12:31 - "And the second is like, namely this, Thou shalt love thy neighbor as thyself. There is none other commandment greater than these."

Parable 19
Obedience

One early morning this man went to town for some business. Now at home his son, who was about 9 years of age, went out into the yard and started cleaning. He cut the grass, cut the trees, raked the yard, and emptied the trash can. Now when the father came home and saw what the boy had done, he was happy, because no one asked or told him to do this. The boy told his father he had put the newspaper on the table. Now some time later two of the boy's friends came over with their bikes. They said to him, "Come with us to fun factory to play some games." The boy told them he had no money. One of the friends said, "Go ask your father." The boy went to his father and asked for $2.00 to play games with his friends. Now the father, knowing what the son did, was pleased with him. How much more will the father give to his son for doing good? Remember how the boy TOLD his father about the newspaper, and now he ASKED his father for something. When you ask, ask it with respect.

Mt. 7:11 - "If ye then, being evil, know how to give good gifts unto your children, how much more shall your Father which is in heaven give good things to them that ask him?"

Parable 20
The Town

Once there was a small town. In the back of this small town was a dirt road.

Some people were in the back of this dirt road. Some of them were sick, some were lame, and some were lost. Then a strong wind came and blew the dirt up like a whirlwind. Now in this dirt was gold dust. The dirt blew away but the gold dust remained. Some people who were sick saw this and said, "Oh my GOD!", and they were then healed.
Some people who were lame said "This is the spirit of GOD!", and could then walk. Some people who were lost had spoken in the spirit. Now this whirlwind lasted for some time, then it fell to the ground and another wind came and covered the gold dust with the dirt. When the spirit of GOD comes, it is you who needs to step out and cry unto GOD.

Jn. 3:8 - "The wind bloweth where it listeth, and thou hearest the sound thereof, but canst not tell whence it cometh, and whither it goeth: so is everyone that is born of the Spirit."

Parable 21
The Lost Boy

In this small valley there was a boy who wasn't too good. He was 15 years of age and at times he took the mail from your mailbox and put it in different mailboxes. At times he let all the air out of your tires. If you caught this boy doing something wrong, he would come back at nighttime and throw rocks at your house, for this boy was not good.

But one day he was riding his bike and there was an old lady walking who slipped and fell. As she was falling, she hit her head on a rock. Now, the boy was riding his bike and happened to be the only one there and he saw what had happened. So he ran to see if he could help the old lady.

Now, there was a man and his family who knew this boy, so they stopped and said to the boy, "What are you doing!?" So he stood up, jumped on his bike and ran away. The man called an ambulance that took the old lady to the hospital, where the old lady fell into a coma.

Now, they caught this boy, and took him to jail and while in jail, he was alone and by himself. The boy said to himself, "I don't know if there is a God and I don't know if God can hear me. I don't even know if I know how to pray. But if there is a God, and if you can hear me, this is one time I have tried to do something good, and they told me if this old lady died they would charge me with murder. But I know between you and me, you know what really happened." Further he asked God, "Can I pray for this one time?" And he said to God, "Forgive me. May I pray for this old lady that you would bring her out of this coma?"

And at the same time in the hospital, the family, her friends, and people in the neighborhood lined around her bed and all held hands and said, "Let's pray unto God for a miracle; for this woman will live." So while they were praying, the old lady came out of the coma. The people jumped for joy and said, "God has heard our voice and he has done this great miracle!"

The old lady said, "It is true that God heard your voices, but it wasn't just your voices. She said to them, "Do you know about the boy that's really bad and is in jail? They said, "Oh, we know what he did to you. We have him locked up!" The old lady said, "No, you don't know what has happened. Neither do you know the truth. For it was his voice that God heard that brought me out of this coma. Go to the boy and set him free."

    Now when the officer went to the jail he said, "The old woman lives. But she said this to you, That God has heard your voice." Now the boy heard that and he knew that he was not alone and that God had heard him. Now I tell you when this boy heard what the man said, he gave his heart to the Lord.

In the Kingdom of God there was great joy, laughter, dancing, and singing, for this boy was lost and now he was found. For it is written, "For the lost shall be found. The captives shall be set free, and also, the truth shall set you free."

The reason why God never heard the other peoples' voices is because they already belonged to God. For this great miracle, God not only saved the boy, but he had saved the old lady. And I'll tell you the truth, this boy was never the same again.

                                            Amen.

Mt. 18:12 - "How think ye? if a man have a hundred sheep, and one of them be gone astray, doth he not leave the ninety and nine, and goeth into the mountains, and seeketh that which is gone astray?"

Parable 22
Faith

What is faith? Faith is to believe. If you ask God for something, you ask him, you do not tell him. So when He's ready to give it to you, He'll give it to you.

There was a man who owned a big field of vegetables and his fruits. Now for three weeks it didn't rain and everything started to die. So that morning he gathered his wife and two kids and said, "Before we eat breakfast, I shall pray unto God." He said, "God, I pray for rain, for if no rain comes my family will starve, so I pray for rain." And after they ate breakfast he was going out the door. And his daughter who was about 11 years old, screamed out to say, "Dad, Dad, have you forgotten something?"

He turned and said, "What is that?" And she said, "Have you not forgotten your raincoat?"

So if you ask God for something, prepare yourself for it. If you prepare yourself, then trust in him to give it to you. In his time, he shall give it to you.

Mt. 17:20 – "...If ye have faith as a grain of a mustard seed, ye shall say unto this mountain, Remove hence to yonder place; and it shall remove; and nothing shall be impossible unto you."

Parable 23
The Face of Jesus

It is written, "For what is a man profited, if he shall gain the whole world, and lose his own soul? or what shall a man give in exchange for his soul?" There once was a man who loved his wife very much. And he had a little girl that was 7 years old. One day he told his wife, "Tomorrow I shall take time off, and we shall go into the country and have a beautiful picnic."

So the next day he, his wife, and his child went on this picnic for which they had made a lot of food. And it was a beautiful day. So they jumped into the van and as they were going through town he said, "I shall stop at the store and buy soda and snacks for the picnic." The man went into the store and left his wife and his daughter in his van. At that moment there was a man robbing the bank next door. As the robber came out of the bank, he went into the man's van and took his wife and his daughter hostage, and he drove far away.

    When the man came out of the store, he noticed that the policemen were there and his van was gone. Now days afterwards, he found out that that man had killed his wife and his daughter. And he said, "When I find this man I shall get revenge for what he has done to my family." So immediately this man stopped going to church, and he developed great hatred in his heart. For nine years he kept on saying the same words, "If I find this man, I shall have my revenge, and I shall kill this man and do what he has done to me."

Now one night his friends came over to visit him at his house. They said, "We have found the man that killed your wife and your daughter. Furthermore, we know where he is staying." So they gave him the address of the house.

Days later he said, "I shall go and get my revenge." And he found out that this man also had a wife and a daughter. So he said, "I shall do unto him what he has done to me." So he parked three or four blocks away from the house and as this man was walking up to the house for revenge that night, he started walking up the stairs. After he had climbed two or three stairs, he heard some noise from inside the bushes and he looked over at them. There was a man that was sitting down there and he had something over his head. The man slowly turned and looked at him, and when he looked at the man, it was Jesus!

    Now Jesus looked into his eyes, and Jesus had tears coming down his face. Right then the man's heart got heavy and his heart began to ache. He knew that if he got revenge on this man, his wife, and his daughter, they would not come back; so he turned around, started to cry, and he walked away. But as he was walking back to his car, he saw a letter on the ground. There was nothing on the envelope, nothing was written. So he picked it up and opened it. The only thing it said inside was, "For now truly you shall see your daughter and your wife in the Kingdom of God."

What is a man who inherits the whole world, but loses his soul? And what shall he give in exchange for his soul? Jesus so loved this man and knew how much he loved his wife and child. So Jesus came down himself and just by the look in Jesus's eyes, he had changed his heart.

Mt. 16:26 - "For what is a man profited, if he shall gain the whole world, and lose his own soul? or what shall a man give in exchange for his soul?"

Acknowledgments

I would like to express my gratitude to the many people who helped me either directly or indirectly in the making of this book; to all those who provided inspiration, support, talked things over, read, offered comments, and assisted in the typing, editing, proofreading and design of this book. Although I am certain I am missing a few names in this very short list, I'd like to especially give my appreciation to the following people:

Pastor Roy Hogan

Matthew Hoflund

Garnie Johnson

Virginia Ramirez

www.ingramcontent.com/pod-product-compliance
Lightning Source LLC
LaVergne TN
LVHW061217060426
835507LV00016B/1973